Sam and the waves

Story by Annette Smith
Illustrations by Pat Reynolds

Sam and Mom
ran down the beach.

They ran down to the water.

"Here comes a wave,"
said Sam.
"Here comes a **big** wave."

"Oh, no!" said Sam.

"The waves are too big!

They are too big for me."

"The waves **are** big, today,"
said Mom.
"Come on, Sam.
Home we go."

Sam and Mom
went back up the beach.

"Look, Mom!" said Sam.

"Can we go in here?"

"The waves are not too big
in here," said Mom.
"You can go in the water."

"And I can see
a little slide!" said Sam.

Sam went up the ladder
and down the little slide.

She went down into the water.

"Look at me!" said Sam.

"I like the **little** waves in here."